The Death Of Money

The Prepper's Guide To Surviving
Economic Collapse, The Loss Of Paper
Assets And How To Prepare When Money
Is Worthless

By Jim Jackson

Disclaimer

This book is intended to be a general guide, to raise awareness, and to help people make informed decisions in the context of their own personal circumstance.

The author accepts no responsibility for any loss or injury be it personal or financial, as a result for the use or misuse of the information in this book. If you have any doubts or concerns after reading this book, please speak to a qualified person before taking any actions.

From The Author

Thank you for taking the time to read this book. As an author, I understand the importance of creating books which my readers will find both enjoyable and informative. If you have the time and feel generous, please don't hesitate to leave an honest review of this book..........Jim Jackson

Table of Contents

Introduction

Chapter 1

Conclusion

Introduction

The economy has experienced instability several times in the past. In fact, if you look at economic history, the UK has experienced at least ten recessions that have hit the country greatly. If you think that an economic crisis is a one-and-done event, that is, the effects won't be experienced now because the crisis was overcome years ago, think again. If you observe the pattern of economic stability from the past through today, you will observe signs of economic downfall, with its seeds sowed and planted deep in our country from ages before. If current economic projections are correct, then the stage has already been set for an economic collapse.

If so, this collapse is inevitable and if you say the economic state of the country is not a major issue for you and you depend on the government leaders to solve the issue, you may be wrong. You can't just blindly trust the leaders of the country, especially when they might not know exactly what they are doing and may not be able to solve the problem. You can't sit back, do nothing and wait on others to find the answers.

In this situation, it is best to be proactive. Though you cannot stop the economic collapse, you can cushion yourself and your family from its effects. One way of doing this is by performing all the necessary preparations. It is not just about preparing for the worst and practicing independence from the system, it is about choosing your own destiny because the economy is in deep shambles.

For those who want to know how to prepare for the upcoming financial collapse, this book is perfect for you. Since the first step in preparing for this catastrophe is to understand what you are preparing for, you will learn about how the financial system works and why it is vulnerable to collapsing in Chapter 1. Next, historical data from other countries will give light to what you can expect when your money becomes worthless. This will be discussed in Chapter 2.

To start off with, Chapter 3 will help you get ready living in a world where money is of little value by teaching you the things you need to prepare for, the skills you need to acquire, and the knowledge on how to strengthen you current position. Chapter 4 will also prepare you for a probable future cash-free economy.

So, I would like to congratulate you for downloading this book. By the end of this read, you will have acquired the information about how you should prepare for an upcoming crisis. So start reading and become the informed and prepared person that you want to be.

Thank you and enjoy!

Chapter 1

The Global Fiat Currency Paradigm And Why Most Fiat Currency's Eventually End Up At Their True Worth

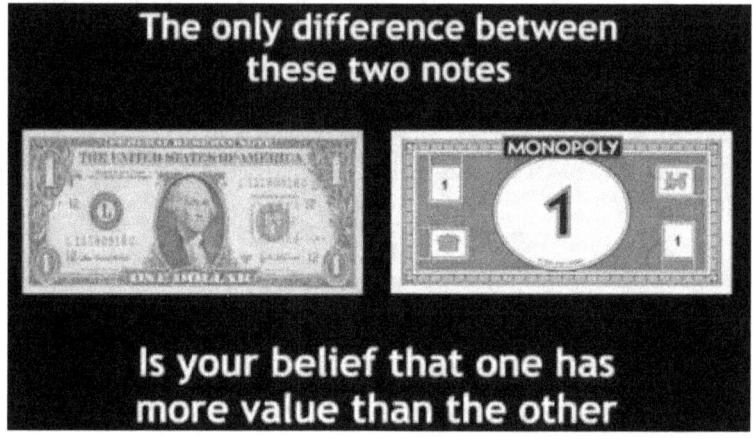

A common sentiment is "history will always repeat itself." We know this, but yet, we still place a great deal of stock in fiat currency. We know fiat currency is essentially worthless, but that doesn't stop countries and governments from putting a great deal of value into a currency without anything to back it up. Fiat currency will not stand the test of time like a piece of gold or silver. Fiat currency is just as fragile as the paper it is printed on. Every paper currency throughout history has fallen. When today's existing fiat falls is not a question of if, but when. In an unprecedented move, all the major economies in the world rely on fiat currency. This is a dangerous situation that will result in a domino effect should a single economy collapse.

Throughout history, we have seen fiat currency fall and become nothing more than tinder for the fire because it truly is paper and nothing more. In fact, the the word fiat means, "it shall be" in Latin. The money is declared to be money by a government. There is nothing to back the money except for word alone. The government is essentially saying they will be good for the money they print. When you think about how shaky the word of our political leaders is, that is more than a little scary.

Fiat currency is born out of central banking as well as supply and demand. There is not a warehouse of gold sitting somewhere to back up the value of that currency. It is backed by word alone. A trip down memory lane will show you how well that has worked out. How many different types of legal tender have been rendered useless and worthless today? The list is quite extensive. Throughout the book, we have talked about some of the governments that have essentially fallen throughout time and along with it, their money.

Take the state of the economy in the United States and in the United Kingdom. Citizens have lost a great deal of faith in their nation's leaders. This is a recipe for disaster and could very well end with each nation's fiat currency falling. Fiat money value is largely based on consumer confidence. Right now, confidence is not high and people are worried.

You should be. Let's talk about fractional reserve lending. This is where things get sketchy. You go to work, get paid and put your money in the bank. The bank is basically borrowing your money. The bank has the right to use the money you deposited to lend to other people, businesses or even invest in the stock market. While your account balance may show your check is still there, it is basically an I.O.U. sitting in your account, not actual currency.

When people take out loans, they are borrowing your money, even though the bank claims it is theirs. Then the loan takers buy their goods and those businesses deposit the money into their account and then their banks loan out that money and so on and so on. When you follow the paper trail of currency, you will find a large stack of I.O.Us in its place, with nothing to back it up. You can see what happens when one person or large business defaults. The domino effect jumps into play and a major economic crash is inevitable.

When things are going along smoothly and citizens are confident their leaders are acting responsibly and leading the government in a good direction, things are great. A booming economy with lots of jobs, standard inflation and manageable taxes are all things citizens appreciate and it will build their trust in their government. The fiat currency is backed by that faith and it will continue to flourish as long as everybody is happy.

It is when things start to get a little shaky and there are signs of big money problems that set off huge warning bells for citizens. Bankers and buyers are citizens and will see the signs. They will get nervous and slow their spending. Again, it is another chain reaction that is set off and things start to get tense. The economy will suffer and the lack of faith translates into a lesser value for the fiat currency. It is almost a given that it will happen, it is just a question of when.

With sluggish economies, governments tend to get a little worried. They can see the house of cards they are sitting atop is shaking and is getting ready to crumble at any moment. What is their option? To make more money to keep the people happy. The printing presses are fired up and the money is put into the economy. More money truly does mean more problems. Now, said country has a lot of paper money floating about for its citizens to use, but other governments know the money means nothing and will quickly refuse to accept the "cash" for payment. Businesses will not be able to buy what they need and will be forced to slow or suspend operations, which means fewer jobs and less money.

Overprinting of money creates hyperinflation. You read about what that means for the economy and the people who are left holding a handful of paper money that is worth less than a roll of toilet paper. Printing more money that has nothing backing it up is a dangerous decision that will have long lasting, devastating consequences. While the intent may have been good, history tells us it will not end well.

The trickle effect will result in banks, lenders and big businesses being paralyzed. The value of the paper money continues to drop, but that doesn't stop more money being made to try and make up for the deficit. It is a dangerous cycle that will only have one outcome—worthless fiat currency. Soon, businesses will stop accepting the paper money altogether. Regular citizens will not be able to buy what they need with paper money and the economy built on that fiat currency will crumble.

Chapter 2

The Possible Causes of Financial Collapse

Knowing the possible causes of economic collapse is helpful to understand the seriousness of its impact and it will also give you additional reasons why preparation is essential. Economic collapse is a phenomenon wherein there is a total breakdown of the national economy, which can result in the unrest of the citizens and produce very high anxiety levels in the population. Below, you will find the possible causes of this financial collapse. Though each of these reasons can solely cause this breakdown, most of the time they co-occur and one cause may be the root of another cause, eventually leading to the crash. In short, the following cases are interrelated and have a causal relationship. You will discover why as you read on.

Causes of Financial Collapse

I.Major Market Crash

Before we delve into what you should do when the market fails, the mechanics of the market will first be explained. The market is a means by which there is an exchange of goods and services as a result of the transaction of buyers and sellers. What is produced, how much of it is produced and the price of a product in a market is a function of the law of supply and demand. This means that when Product A is in demand, producers will want to make more of it and so its price will increase. On the other hand, if the consumers lose their interest in Product A, the supply will be more than the demand. This will then create a surplus (excess goods), which will make the price go down.

The stock market is similar to the market discussed above, though it has only one specific product – stocks or shares. These two terms are essentially the same and refer to a share of ownership in the company. If you have a percentage of stock in a company, you will be entitled to the same percentage of the assets and earnings of that company.

Following the law of supply and demand, if the stocks of a company look promising, its prices will be set high and people will compete to buy these stocks. When the company looks shaky, people will compete to sell their stocks to the highest bidder, even if it means selling it at a lower price than their original purchasing price.

If you are not an investor in the stock market or do not take part in the stock market activities, then you are probably dying to skip this part. However, you need to know that stock markets have a major impact on the economy and their impact will reach you no matter how immune you think you are.

When things are looking good for a company and it seems like it has a potential for growth, investors will put so much demand on the stocks that they will drive the price of the stock higher. Sometimes, the price will increase so much that it exceeds the true value of the company, which can create a "bubble". The price will continue to increase beyond its actual worth and since it is not grounded on anything substantial, that "bubble" will eventually pop. When that "bubble" pops, it is bad news. What happens is that the investors will be *panic selling*, that is, they will try to get out of the business as soon as they can by selling their stocks.

Panic selling is the most common cause of a financial collapse and it is grounded mainly on fear. The investors will forget to evaluate the situation objectively, so they will sell at any price to avoid further loss. Even more damaging is that panic selling has a spiral affect, and that spiral is more likely to go down. When investors see that others are selling their stocks and prices are rapidly fluctuating, they interpret this as a sign to get out of business. As more and more investors sell their stocks, the lower the price of the stocks become and it will fall. This fluctuation of stock prices results in a financial collapse.

II.**Hyper Inflation**

If you think that hyperinflation is just inflation raised to some degree, then you are absolutely wrong. Inflation is a phenomenon wherein the prices of goods rise while the purchasing power of your dollars decrease because there is an increase in money supply. The rate of inflation will be the rate by which the price of goods rises in a given market.

Hyper inflation, on the other hand, is much more drastic than inflation. Here, the value of your dollar declines so rapidly that it will mean nothing in just a matter of days or months. There are usually two precedents of hyperinflation.

•Increase in money supply. As you may already know, the currencies we are using right now are nothing but paper. It is not grounded on any gold or other substance with true value. So basically, the government can print all the money it wants. When released into the economy, the freshly printed crisp money dilutes the value of the money already in existence. Reiterating the point on the law of supply and demand, the more the supply of a good or service, the lower its price or value will be.

•Loss of faith in the currency. For hyperinflation to occur there should be uncertainty of the worth of currency. This is when people start to trade their cash for things with actual utility and value, say gold and precious metals. People try to get rid of the paper money because the currency becomes something that no one is interested anymore.

If either or both of these two occur, what happens next is that the sellers will set the price for the useful goods embarrassingly high to discourage the consumers from buying and to turn them away. Why would the businesses sell today when the currency they will receive will be worth nothing?

The distinction between inflation and hyperinflation should be clearer now. You now know how scary hyperinflation can be. What's scarier is that it can happen to us and is a dark ominous cloud hanging over our heads.

I.Deflation

Deflation is the opposite of inflation. It is defined as the contraction in the total supply of money and credit, which results in a decrease in the price of goods and commodities. The causes of deflation are as follows.

•**Consumers lack the liquidity to fuel consumption**. When people have a strict budget, say for instance, their salary or wage is unchanging; they will try to cut down their expenses. This will cause them to consume less and save more.

•**Stricter credit**. If banks and other lending companies enforce stricter credit rules, this can result to harder credit applications and higher interest rates. This will cause people to decrease their purchases since it will entail higher interests.

•**Demand is not keeping up with supply**. Thanks to technology, factories are producing at their maximum level to put goods in the market. But, because consumers have cut down their expenses and credit becomes unavailable, these goods go unsold resulting in global excess capacity. To avoid the waste of these goods, sellers decrease their selling price to invite costumers to buy more.

You might think that prices going down are something good, but that is not the case. If at the time of production prices were still high, but at when the product is sold the prices are cheaper, the companies will experience a loss. In order to recover, they would have to stop hiring, lay off workers and avoid extra costs. They don't have to produce much anyway. This will cause the unemployment rate to rise. In addition, when people are aware of the current trend in the economy where there is constant deflation, they are more likely to postpone buying until the next day thinking that the prices will become cheaper. These actions can lead to the downward spiral of economy.

I. Natural Disasters

Natural disasters do not only damage houses and the environment, but can also damage the economy and cause a financial collapse. Listed below are several effects that natural disasters such as hurricane, tornadoes and earthquakes can have on the economy.

•**Stock market crash**. Natural disasters can be an indication for loss of business or bad business. This causes investors to sell their stocks and start a spiralling effect, causing other investors to sell their stocks too. This, as you already know, results to panic selling and the decrease in price of stocks. The ill effects of panic selling, which may be brought about by natural disasters, can cause a market crash.

•**Increase in the price of commodities**. Natural disasters can also result in the decrease in supply of commodities as crops are washed out and manufacturing companies are closed. This can result in a general increase in the prices of commodities and inflation.

•The government has to release money in the economy. As it is the duty of the government to step up and help the people, they will release money to the economy. They will provide money for building materials, first aid and food for the people. The people will gladly accept the financial assistance released by the government to help them recover from the calamity without knowing the repercussions of the influx of money in the economy. As long as the financial assistance does not go overboard, the economy will have a chance to recover in time.

Based on the effects stated above, natural disasters can be followed by inflation, hyper inflation and stock market crash, then consequently a financial collapse. Although the economy can crash without the help of natural disasters, these disasters can, however, act like fuel for the collapse. It is dreadful to know that we might be expecting more natural disasters to hit us now. The world is experiencing more intense storms as the climate is rapidly changing. Earthquakes become more frequent as we run the water tables dry. We are on the verge of environmental crisis and when these natural disasters hit us, financial collapse is sure to follow.

Chapter 3

What You Can Expect If Your Money Becomes Worthless

When the time of economic collapse eventually arrives, every economy and every country is at risk because they all have a monetary system that uses Fiat currencies. They are merely paper with prints of numbers, and gold or any other substance of real value do not back up them up. Since its birth in China hundreds of years ago, inflation and depreciation of value are already part of its features. In the event of an economic collapse, especially one that is brought about by hyperinflation, paper money will surely be reduced to what it really is, which is just paper with no real value. For a concrete picture of what you can expect when your money becomes worthless, enumerated herein are some countries that have already experienced it and the events, which led them to experience it.

The Historical Precedents

You have already learned that printing too much money is the number one cause of it losing its value. But why do governments feel the need to print more money? Based on the data from countries that experienced hyperinflation, there are two reasons why governments overprint money: war and a collapse in production.

Wars are extremely costly. Not only does it cost lives, but people's money as well, because in order to win, the government needs to provide for an army, acquire weaponry, and build an armoury. A collapse in production, on the other hand, can result to hyperinflation, as there is only a little supply and a high demand for goods and services. When there is a shortage in food, for example, suppliers will increase the price of food and peg them extremely high. The government, taking intervention, will release money into the economy causing the value to fluctuate. Enumerated below are countries whose economy was devastated because of wars and the dwindling of production.

•**Germany**. Germany had to abandon their gold standard and print more currency to finance the war during the First World War. But then, Germany lost and had to pay reparations to various countries such as France and

A 1923 50 Million German Mark Printed During The Weimar Republic's Period Of Hyperinflation

Belgium. France and the other countries have demanded from them a total of 132 billion gold marks (more than 52 billion in today's pounds). With its factories in ruin and production capacity significantly reduced, there was no way the country could repay its debt. So Germany's central bank, Reichsbank, issued massive amount of marks and further went beyond their gold standard. Their monetary explosion and loss of faith in the currency resulted to severe hyperinflation in 1922. They had an inflation rate of 322% per month. To be exact, the price of commodities doubled every 3.7 days.

•**Bosnia & Herzegovina**. When the country became independent from Yugoslavia in 1992, a civil war erupted between its three cultural divisions namely Serbs, Bosniak and Croats. Their bloody civil war has disrupted and displaced most of their population and their

A Bosnian 100,000,000 dinar Note From 1923

economy went down in shambles. Their currency, then the Bosnian dinar, was very unstable and plunged in value. In 1992, the highest denomination was 1000 dinars, which became 100,000,000 dinars in 1993.

•**Hungary**. A larger hyperinflation occurred in Hungary after the Second World War. Because of the destruction of resources from the war, the price of goods became higher than before so the government increased the supply of money for people not to starve. Consequently, from August 1945 to July 1946, the prices of goods rose at a shocking rate of 19000% per

A Man Sweeping Up Hungarian Bank Notes In 1946 After The Hungarian Pengo Was Replaced

month. It even reached to a point where prices tripled each day in July 1946.

•**Zimbabwe**. From 2004 to 2009, Zimbabwe experienced hyperinflation. This was due to their government printing too much money to fund the war in Congo. Moreover, the hyperinflation was intensified by the

A Man Carting Around Zimbabwean Bank Notes In a Wheelbarrow During Zimbabwe's Period Of Inflation

drought and farm confiscation, which limited their food supply. This resulted in a hyperinflation even worse than that of Germany, their prices doubled every 24 hours!

So, when your money becomes worthless, you can expect that there will be nothing cheap enough to buy with it. As these countries above have experienced, the only thing you can do to get out of that situation is adopt a new currency, but history always repeats itself, and any new currency will not be an exception to the natural downward spiral of its value.

Chapter 4

Living In World Where Money Is Of Little Value

Money is something that has been used for a long time to make people's lives easier and transactions consistent. However, since inflation and its depreciating value are already part of its features, we can expect its worth to be reduced to nothing. When that happens, even if you have a lot of money, a trip to the grocery store will be futile because even a bag full of cash will not be worth a single piece of gum anymore and if you think this is all there is in an economic collapse, think hard again. Those who have resources like food, land, and water will hoard them, crimes will become rampant, people will fight to sustain themselves and their loved ones, and if you do not know how to take care of yourself and your family, you will most likely suffer hunger, danger, pain, fear, and hopefully not, death.

In that case, how can you survive? To have any chance of survival, specified below are the tips on how to strengthen your current position, the skills you need to acquire, and the things you need to stockpile to prepare for the future.

Strengthening Your Position

The fact that the world is a battleground will be cemented when economic collapse comes through. We have been in competition with each other since childhood, even without things like inflation rates and prices bothering us. When we are faced by a collapsing economy, these competitions will be further intensified. The only way we won't lose the battle is by strengthening our current position in the following ways.

•**Be indispensable in the company you are working for.** An economic crash, no matter how slight, can entail mass layoffs. Surely you are aware of times when a number of people became unemployed as the company they were working for were forced to shut down or implement mass layoffs to cut down costs. If somebody or a corporation currently employs you, then you are in jeopardy of being laid off. You can avoid this by being an indispensable asset to your company, no matter what the nature of the business is. Do your best in your job, prove your worth to your company, do everything you can in every ethical way possible to hold on to your position. Even better, be self-employed. With this, you won't have to worry about a boss or being laid off.

•**Start a garden**. Our global food reserves are at its lowest and the ever-changing weather conditions are certainly not helping. The facts are, you should have your own access to food. By starting your own garden now, it won't make you so reliant on the system, and when the inevitable comes, you won't have to compete for the limited food supply that seven billion people will also be fighting for.

•**Earn friends**. Though earning friends will indeed give you more mouths to feed, you will also have more hands to feed you. In other words, earning friends can become an asset. Aside from the social support they will provide at difficult times, you can barter with them to help all of you survive.

•**Invest safely**. If ever you will find yourself with extra money and are thinking of investing it in the stock market, the safest way to proceed is by investing it in a company that is already established and has a proven track record. The rule is that you should buy low and sell high. You might not get your return as early as you want, but you will be getting something. It is much riskier to invest in the "what's in" right now because chances are, most people are investing in it and it will cost more than it is truly worth and when your "bubble" pops, all the money that you invested will go down the drain!

The Skills You Need To Learn

Basically, the things enumerated below are the skills you need to acquire so that you can be independent from the system. Being system independent does not mean that you shouldn't trust the government; this means that you should be able to survive on your own without the system. Here is how you can do that:

•**Gardening skills**. Learning this skill is important for reasons that you surely already know. When the grocery stores and supermarkets close, the only people who will have something to eat for a sustained period of time are farmers and gardeners. Owners of grocery stores may indeed have abundance of food supplies for a few months but they won't last and owners won't be able to replenish their stocks. Soon enough, the jars of peanut butter or canned meat will expire, leaving them with nothing to eat. Therefore, it should be everybody's business to grow his or her own food. Start right now by planting some vegetables and fruit trees in your backyard. Also, include herbs and other medicinal plants. There are many books available to guide you on how to grow your own garden even if you do not have a green thumb. One important thing to remember, you should keep your prepping to yourself or people will know whom to go when they don't have anything to eat. Though helping is good, you must place the safety of your family first.

•**Self-defense**. If you have watched documentaries about economic crisis, then you have probably noticed that crime and riots dramatically increase and worsen in those times and when the economy truly collapses, more riots and violence will surely crop up. There will be unrest in major cities and there will be looters everywhere. If you have priceless goods such as fuel and food and everybody in your community knows that, then you will become a magnet for thieves. If so, you should know how to defend yourself, your family and your property by then. You can start by learning how to use a gun and practicing hand to hand combat.

•**First aid**. Doctors can still be in business during a financial collapse. The problem will be how you can pay them since they will no longer be accepting cash. You barter resources for their services, sure, but it would still be better to have a doctor in your family, or someone who knows medicine. But the most basic skill you and everyone in your family must have is first aid. It is such an invaluable skill in your daily life and will more so during an economic collapse. This skill is very helpful in emergency situations and could spell the difference between life and death. You also need to familiarize yourself on appropriate medicines for common illnesses. You don't have to be a doctor to learn this skill. You can just enroll yourself in a First Aid Course and learn about medicines you might need. To supplement your knowledge, First Aid books will be very helpful to you, too.

•**Turning what you know into a business**. It is better to be self-employed. You should not rely so much on the company you are working for because when an economic collapse strikes, there's a great chance that it will wipe you out with it. So it would be best to start a little business. For example, if you know how to bake or cook, why don't you start it as a *side-line* business? You can bake cupcakes and sell them to your colleagues at work, in that way, you earn extra money. When the time you most dread arrives and people start looking everywhere for something to eat, you can exchange your baked goods with other valuable resources as well.

What You Need To Stockpile

We don't know exactly when the economy will collapse, but one thing's for sure – its condition is worsening as the years pass and it is not showing a sign of recovery. When the day comes that everything we have known to be essential parts of our lives are closing, when groceries, supermarkets, boutiques and malls are one-by-one being shut down, how do you plan to survive? Here are some things you need to get and start adding to your stockpile for you to have a larger chance of survival.

•**Water**. It is basic fact that approximately 65% of the human body is made up of water and there is no way your body can generate its own water. This means you need to keep yourself hydrated if you are to survive. No one can last long without water, so this should be part of your emergency supply. It is suggested you keep at least four 5-gallon water containers in your household and fill it with drinking water to help you last you long enough until you get your bearings. Also, devise a plan that will help you acquire more clean drinking water when disaster strikes. You can do this by preparing water purification tablets and water bottles with filter. With these, water in streams will be as good as the drinking water you are used to.

•**Food**. This goes together with water. You need much of the food stored in order to function properly, and thus survive. Having a garden is not enough. You should make sure to stockpile food, choosing those with long shelf lives such as white rice, preserved or canned fruits and vegetables, canned meat, flour, mixed beans, frozen olive oil, nutrition bars and peanut butter with the expiry date of at least two years, the longer the better. You can add foods of your choice, together with these suggestions. Just make sure that your food supplies are enough to support you and your family for at least six months or more.

•**Precious metals**. When the value of your paper money dies, precious metals such as gold and silver may still hold value. Gold and silver are excellent trade items and can work even during a financial crisis, so it is imperative that you have some of these precious metals stored in your secret safe in case you have to trade them for something you might need.

•**Alternative sources of energy**. Should the power grid go down, you need to devise a plan to get electricity without being very reliant to the power company. It may take days or weeks for the power grid to be functional again or it may no longer be in business at all. So you should start preparing things as an alternative you can use when this happens. Solar panels, rechargeable batteries, and solar rechargers should be part of your stockpile. Also include matches, lamp oil, firewood and the like so that you could use something for cooking. Lastly, never forget flashlights and extra batteries for each member of the family.

•**First aid kit**. You should be able to tend for yourself and your family in emergency medical situations, and a ready first aid kit will be very helpful. Your first aid kit must contain bandages, alcohol, povidone-iodine solution, cotton swabs, ointments, scissors and the like. You must also include in your first aid kit, medicines for common illnesses like flu, cough, colds, headaches, stomach pains, and etc. Also, include vitamins and minerals because you cannot afford to be sick and risk your health in critical situations like an economic meltdown.

•**Clothes and personal hygiene supply**. These are the things, which most people don't take into account when prepping. Remember that your hygiene significantly affects your health, so you must not miss your hygiene products. You must also invest in blankets and durable clothes to get help you get through extreme weather conditions, like heavy snow, long periods of rain, and heat. Also, grab a pair of good hiking boots and running shoes, while you are at it, you might as well prepare those now.

•**Communication devices**. You will be lucky if phones and the internet can still be used by the time the economy crashes down. But, the opposite is more likely. If so, a radio will do to keep you updated of the conditions outside. A handheld radio-transmitter or a walkie-talkie will also be helpful communication if ever lines are down.

•**Guns and ammunition**. Having guns and ammunition may be too much and too drastic for you, but they are necessary. Though there is a possibility that an economic collapse will not be as bad as it seems and there is a chance that weapons will not be necessary, it won't hurt you to be prepared. For example, if by chance, other people know that you have a stockpile of food, water and precious resources when they do not have any, you can be a target of hungry neighbours, thieves, criminals and other people. They will, by all means, also want to survive as much as you do. Although you might dread the thought of other people attacking you, it is a great possibility in an economic collapse. When this happens, you need to be able to protect you and your family and secure your survival. I suggest you start oiling your guns and collect ammunitions as much as you can.

•**A getaway vehicle.** You may ask yourself, "Why would I need a getaway vehicle for?" No, economic collapse is not a zombie apocalypse, but when things take a turn for the worse and societal collapse follows the financial collapse, having your own vehicle might be your chance of escape to a more stable country or city. You might as well secure your passports in your vehicle and some food as well. In case escaping is not necessary, having your own car will be useful to get more resources and make important trips. See to it that your car always has a full tank and that you have extra gasoline and diesel. Also, make sure that you regularly maintain your vehicle and that it is in a proper condition or it might not get you anywhere.

Chapter 5

Cash Free Economics

Because its value has been rapidly decreasing over the years, it will soon become impossible to survive if the only thing you hold onto is your monetary wealth. However, even though ancestral societies have succeeded making transactions without cash before, going back to a cash-free economy won't be that simple. Trading and bartering is a useful know-how if you want to survive in a cash free economy, though this can be a bit hard at first because we have been used to using money and our ideas of what is truly important and useful have changed. It would then be very difficult to agree upon a good, which would be as valuable as that something you want to have. In simple words, it would be harder to make people satisfied with an exchange. Nonetheless, to help you deal with this, you can learn about the things you can invest in and ways on how to barter.

Things Worth Investing In

Now that money still holds some value, might as well use it for things you might need when the economy collapses. The things mentioned above that you need to stockpile are related to the things suggested here.

•**Precious metals**. When the paper money fails, the society will definitely go back to the time when we trade goods via precious metals. While the prices of gold and silver are still low,

While The Price Of Precious Metals Fluctuates In The Short Term, Long Term Fiat Currencies Will Always Depreciate In Value Whilst Precious Metals Will Generally Maintain Their Value

you better invest on them now and you will never regret it when you can buy milk and bread with your silver and gold in the future.

•**Coins**. Never downplay the importance of coins just because they have little value to you now. When the pound depreciates to nothing, it will become just a printed-paper and nothing more. However, you can

Old Coins Can Be A Great Long Term Investment As Not Only Are They Usually Rarer And Therefore More Collectable But Many Older Coins Also Contained Precious Metals In Them Such As Gold Or Silver

still buy with your coins, since coins are also made up of metals, which can be melted and forged to something people can use. You should start finding those jars of coins passed on to you by your dad or search your bags for forgotten changes. Keep them in a safer place and save them for the future.

●**Food**. May it be a garden with vegetables, a coop with chickens, a pond with fishes, or a room full of dry goods, invest in anything that can give you access to food. Having food will be your greatest advantage as it is the most basic of human needs. People may  lose taste for precious metals, but people will never lose taste for food. Food can also be a very good product for trading.

How To Barter

Gold is a symbol of civilization and trade. Our ancestors have been using gold for thousands of years to stand for the cash that we now use. But when civilizations and trades break down, all that is left to do is barter. Barter is the exchange of goods and services directly without the use of any currencies. In times like an economic collapse, barter is very useful as it ensures the flow of necessary items into the household without using money. For instance, a man with a cow will perhaps give you some milk in exchange for the bread you baked, or you can barter a gallon of water for a pack of canned goods.

In a tough economy, you will need to learn how to barter. Here are some tips you can use while bartering:

•**Know the value of the item you will barter.** You should know what your item is worth before bartering it. A thing doesn't necessarily have to be worthless to you for you to barter it. It may also mean that you have an excess supply of the resource or you need something, which ranks greater in importance. You should be willing to give an item up to be able to get another, which is more important to you.

•**Know what you want.** You don't want to waste what you have for things you won't need or things that are not worth the product you are willing to give, so you have to decide on the resources you really want to get. If you want a fresh loaf of bread, do not settle for a moldy roll just because the person on the other end of the transaction thinks that that is what your item is worth. If you really know the true value of your item and that it's worth even two fresh loaves of bread, stand your ground and be firm. Soon enough, that person will give in. Besides, he/she won't start a deal with you if he/she doesn't also need what you are willing to offer.

•**Be stoic.** When the trader sees that you are badly interested in the object he offers, chances are, he would demand more for it. You should act casual and impassive and try not to look very interested in making the deal.

•**Don't bring other valuable items.** If you do not intend to barter them, do not bring them or you will regret exchanging them for things you do not need using those few valuable items.

•**Don't be afraid to ask questions**. You might want to ask how his solar flashlights are used, if it's still in good condition, or how long it has been used. Never be afraid to ask these questions so you don't end up with a poor barter.

•**Test the items to make sure they work**. Before you end the transaction, test the item first in front of the person you are transacting with. If it works fine, you can both call it a finished deal. But, if the item is not working, then you still have a chance to cancel. This will also give you and your trade partner an opportunity to learn more about the products that you both want to get.

Conclusion

Congratulations! You have now reached the final page this eBook, "The Death Of Money"

By this time, I hope you have an understanding of economic collapse and understanding the economic system and current problems the economy is facing. You have also learned about the things you must do to strengthen your current position, the valuable skills you need to master and prepare, and other important knowledge to help you start your prepping.

The future may look bleak right now and the idea of chaos when an economic collapse will come is very disturbing, but it is not a reason to panic. In fact, this is the right time to pause, think and prepare. By reading this book, you already have the advantage of preparation, the ultimate weapon of survival in times of crises.

And so, I hope this book has taught you many things about preparing for a future economic collapse.
Thank you and congratulations again for downloading this book!

Other Book By Jim Jackson

Prepper's Pantry

Are you prepared in the event of an emergency? Do you have ample food storage to keep your family fed during a disaster? If not, then this book will guide you through the process of preparing for anything. These first steps in preparing your pantry will give you peace of mind knowing that you did what was necessary to care for your family. In this easy-to-read guide you will find information and facts you may have never considered and will gather valuable resources to sustain your family. The Prepper's  Pantry can be the starting point for making sure your family can survive.

Camping And Cooking For Beginners

Everyone has a camping disaster story and rarely do they have anything to do with wild animals. From forgetting the food to discovering the tent is too small—a myriad of things can go wrong, but with Camping And Cooking For Beginners , your problems are solved. Beginning with the basics, this handy helper starts with a checklist of what you need for your trip. Choosing the right tent, the right sleeping bag and how to start fires without matches (and he's not talking about rubbing two sticks together!) are only a few chapters in the book. The best advice is the authors Top Ten Mistakes First Time Campers Make (and how to avoid them!)—it is invaluable. Get your copy today, before your camping trip and transform your camping experience into the best memory ever!

Motorhome Living For Beginners

When you want to change your lifestyle entirely, you need to have enough motivation but you also need to have knowledge about the lifestyle that you are adopting. Many people who want to live in an RV full-time fail to find a balance in their lives which make that living pleasurable, while others can live the dream and learn to compromise on comforts for the sake of freedom. They wake up in the mornings to feel that they have breathed fresh air. They see different scenery every morning if they so wish. What you need to know before joining them is whether you're cut out for the lifestyle and what differences there are between living in a conventional home and living in an RV. This book bridges that gap in your knowledge, and although you may choose to save a fortune by staying at home, you may also choose the lesser traveled road and discover the benefits of living in an RV.

Both lifestyles, either in an RV or a home, have their pros and cons. Many who choose the RV lifestyle find that adapting their lives comes naturally. It takes a unique and free spirited person to compromise on the luxuries of home living in favor of the adventurous lifestyle offered by RV living, though many do. Once you weigh the pros and cons, you can make the choice wisely, and that's what this book is all about. The book will appeal to the free spirited who seek something more than merely surviving month to month oppressed by mortgage payments and housing taxes.

Both have benefits, though those who live the life they choose, rather than the life chosen for them by responsibility, find that RV life tests their personal boundaries and skills freeing up their lives to live beyond the grid. Journey with us and learn if living in an RV will suit you, and be prepared for the journey of your life.

www.ingramcontent.com/pod-product-compliance
Lightning Source LLC
Chambersburg PA
CBHW071343310526
45790CB00018B/1221